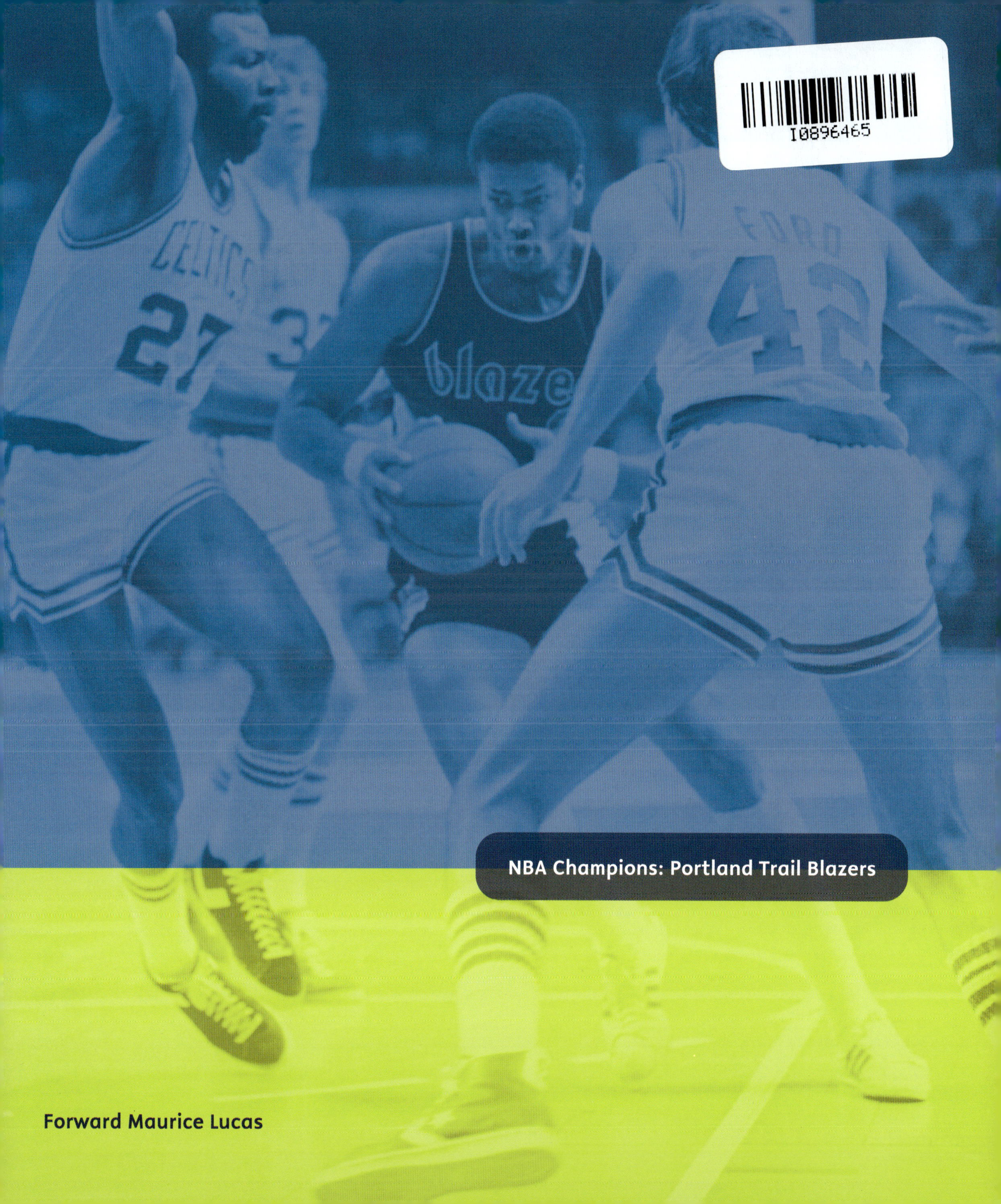

NBA Champions: Portland Trail Blazers

Forward Maurice Lucas

Guard Brandon Roy

NBA CHAMPIONS

PORTLAND TRAIL BLAZERS

DENNY BULCAO, JR.

CREATIVE EDUCATION / CREATIVE PAPERBACKS

Center Bill Walton

Published by Creative Education and Creative Paperbacks
P.O. Box 227, Mankato, Minnesota 56002
Creative Education and Creative Paperbacks are imprints of
The Creative Company
www.thecreativecompany.us

Art Direction by Tom Morgan
Book production by Graham Morgan
Edited by Grace Cain

Images by Alamy Stock Photo/ ZUMA Press, 24; Associated Press/ ED KOLENOVSKY, 19; Getty Images/ Andrew D. Bernstein, 16, Ezra Shaw, cover, Focus On Sport, cover, 3, 4, Jayne Kamin-Oncea, 10, Joe Murphy, 2, Lauren Sopourn, 20, Layne Murdoch, 5, Sam Forencich, 7, 12, Thomas Oliver, 6, Walter Iooss Jr. 15; Paul Benoit, 1; Unsplash/ Adam Blank, 9

Library of Congress Cataloging-in-Publication Data
Names: Bulcao, Denny Jr., author.
Title: Portland Trail Blazers / by Denny Bulcao Jr.
Description: Mankato, Minnesota : Creative Education and Creative Paperbacks, [2025] | Series: Creative sports: NBA champions | Includes index. | Audience: Ages 7-10 | Audience: Grades 2-3 | Summary: "Elementary-level text and dynamic sports photos highlight the NBA championship win of the Portland Trail Blazers, plus sensational players associated with the professional basketball team such as Anfernee Simons"— Provided by publisher.
Identifiers: LCCN 2024014028 (print) | LCCN 2024014029 (ebook) | ISBN 9798889892649 (library binding) | ISBN 9781682776308 (paperback) | ISBN 9798889893752 (ebook)
Subjects: LCSH: Portland Trail Blazers (Basketball team)—History—Juvenile literature. | Basketball players—United States—Juvenile literature.
Classification: LCC GV885.52.P67 B85 2025 (print) | LCC GV885.52.P67 (ebook) | DDC 796.323/640979549—dc23/eng/20240405
LC record available at https://lccn.loc.gov/2024014028
LC ebook record available at https://lccn.loc.gov/2024014029

Printed in China

Center Greg Oden

Forward Rudy Fernández

CONTENTS

Home of the Trail Blazers

Portland, Oregon, is located across the Columbia River from Washington. It is near the Cascade mountain range in the Pacific Northwest. The city has an **arena** called Moda Center. It is the home of the Trail Blazers basketball team.

Guard Damian Lillard

The Portland Trail Blazers are a National Basketball Association (NBA) team. They compete in the Northwest Division. That is part of the Western Conference. Two of their biggest **rivals** are the Denver Nuggets and the Los Angeles Lakers. All NBA teams want to win the **NBA Finals** and become champions.

Guard Brandon Roy

Naming the Trail Blazers

In the 1800s, some people traveled across the country on the Oregon Trail in covered wagons. Many of them settled in what is now Oregon. Those early settlers "blazed a trail." That means they made a new path through wildlands.

Trail Blazers History

The Trail Blazers started playing in 1970. They had six losing seasons. New coach Jack Ramsay built a winning team around center Bill Walton. Walton was a great passer and shot blocker. He stood 6 feet, 11 inches.

Walton and forward Maurice Lucas led the Trail Blazers to the **playoffs** in 1977. They lost the first two games of the Finals against the Philadelphia 76ers. Then they won four games in a row. The team became champions in just their seventh

Center Bill Walton

Swingman Clyde Drexler

season! Walton was named **Most Valuable Player (MVP)** of the NBA the next season.

Starting in 1983, the Blazers made the playoffs 21 seasons in a row. Star **swingman** Clyde Drexler was nicknamed "Clyde the Glide." Portland reached the Finals again in 1990 and 1992. They lost both times.

The Trail Blazers didn't make the playoffs for five straight years in the 2000s. Center-forward LaMarcus Aldridge led Portland back to the playoffs in 2009.

Other Trail Blazers Stars

The Trail Blazers have been led by terrific guards. Geoff Petrie was the Blazers' first star in the 1970s. Terry Porter ran the offense in the 1980s and '90s. Guards Damian Lillard and C. J. McCollum averaged 50 points per game together for three seasons.

Guard Geoff Petrie

Center Deandre Ayton

High-jumping forward Jerome Kersey was known for his power dunks. Rasheed Wallace made the **All-Star team** two times as a Trail Blazer.

The current team leaders are shooting guard Anfernee Simons and center Deandre Ayton. Fans hope they will soon help the Trail Blazers win a second championship.

About the Trail Blazers

First season: 1970–71

Conference/division: Western Conference, Northwest Division

Team colors: red, black, and white

Home arena: Moda Center

NBA CHAMPIONSHIPS:

1977, 4 games to 2 over Philadelphia 76ers

TEAM WEBSITE:

https://www.nba.com/blazers/

Glossary

All-Star team—a special team made up of the best players in each NBA conference

arena—a large building with seats for spectators, where sports games and entertainment events are held

Most Valuable Player (MVP)—an honor given to the season's best player

NBA Finals—a series of games between two teams at the end of the playoffs; the first team to win four games is the champion

playoffs—games that the best teams play after a regular season to see who the champion will be

rival—a team that plays extra hard against another team

swingman—a basketball player who can play guard or forward

Guard Damian Lillard

Index